Search Me

A Four-Week Study of God's Redemptive Plan in Psalm 139

Written by

Mandi Cornett

and

Maggie Cornett

Table of Contents

Search Me

Opening Thoughts

Welcome to… Search Me. We are excited to spend this time with you, journeying through Psalm 139. As we write, it is winter and Maggie and I are literally snowed into a little house nestled in the woods of Northwestern Indiana.

Earlier, we had a terrible time getting up a steep hill in the middle of a snow storm—my car just couldn't make it. We slid down the hill and almost hit a mail box along the way! It was scary, frustrating, and frankly, a very annoying situation. We were trying to get somewhere for an important task…the task of writing this study! But, the car and the weather were "in charge," it seemed, and we were helpless…. until we were helped. My husband came to the rescue! Whew! We were saved!

When we finally arrived home to our little house, my thoughts turned to the correlation of this frustrating event to our study. I had a plan that I couldn't control. I tried to be brave and help myself, but I was helpless and hopeless without the help of another. And, in the middle of it all, my emotions went haywire! Does that sound familiar?

I don't know about you, but for me and yes, even 15-year-old Maggie, it sounds a lot like everyday life. Plans don't go our way. We don't feel seen, known, or acknowledged, we feel alone and helpless and we need help. Intellectually, we may know that our help comes from the Lord. However, if I'm honest, I often look for help in a lot of other places first when life leaves me feeling stranded on a snowy hill, sliding downwards.

Psalm 139 is a fantastic reminder of the truth of God's character, His care and His ability to redeem everything, including our downward slides. We will look carefully at this Psalm and several interwoven threads of Scripture and we'll unpack some beautiful truths of God's great redemptive plan.

This is the first study written by both of us and I'm honored to introduce you to my daughter, Maggie. She's smart, funny, beautiful and full of 15-year-old sass! Being her mom is a great honor, challenge (at times!) and a tremendous joy. But, what thrills my heart the most is that she is my sister in the Lord. We are a mother-daughter duo until one of us dies, but we are sisters, in Christ, for eternity. I love her part of the Body of Christ and I'm sure you will, too. Thank you for joining us.

Our prayer is that this resource will help you dig into the Word of God and that you'll be challenged to think about and be called into a deep walk with Jesus and others. We pray that this workbook will help and encourage you to change. Each week there will be seven prompts:

Searching the Word: This is your study time. Each week there will be a series of texts that will thread through Scripture. This is a time for you to pause, pray, read, and observe as you prayerfully study the Word. You will read each text from two versions of the Bible. Take time to mark a few words and answer corresponding questions from the text.

Seen by a Teen: These are some thoughts, insights and transparent questions that Maggie, my 15-year-old daughter, wants to share with you. We've embarked on this journey through Psalm 139 together and I'm excited for you to hear from her.

Ponder: Each week you will spend time considering and thinking through the "Ponder" questions of the week. These are not questions you necessarily need to answer, but they are good prompts to simply get you thinking.

Pulling together: If you have the time, each week you'll be encouraged to review the texts of the week and look at a series of "big picture" questions.

Keepsakes: Each week you will be encouraged to write out and memorize a verse of the week, getting it into your heart.

Sharing your heart: This prompt will encourage you to pray and process with the Lord.

Reach out: Finally, each week we'll encourage you to apply, possibly act, and share a truth you are learning, in order to incorporate these truths into your everyday life.

There is nothing particularly special about this workbook. We simply mean to encourage you to dig into God's Word, into these truths, any way you can. Don't get thrown off by the workbook; simply spend time in God's Word; I promise, you will not be the same!

We pray this resource will be a tool in His Hand, to guide, teach and challenge you to find your value, worth and purpose in Christ alone. We pray that you will learn to stand strong as your part in what He is creating: His Body and Bride. We pray that you will see what He sees and know that you are known.

Pray with me: "Oh Jesus, give us eyes to see You clearly and to see who we are in You. Soften our hearts to receive the beauty and grace of your Redemption. Grow in us Your likeness, in Your time and in Your way. Give us eyes to see what You see and love what You love. Grow our eyes of faith in You and Your finished work. In Jesus name, Amen."

Thank you for joining us. We're excited to grow with you!

Known to know Him more and more, with you…

Maggie and Mandi Cornett

Let's stay connected! Find me on Facebook!

Mandi.cleansefillpour@gmail.com

www.mandicornett.com

Week 1:

Our God...Who Sees and Knows You

Our God sees and knows us. That is what Psalm 139 is all about. He is the God who sees, knows, and is able to do anything. There is great comfort in that, but honestly, there can also be great confusion. Why doesn't He change certain circumstances? People? Why doesn't He change me?

Sometimes, if I'm honest, I want a god who will swoop in and make everything fairytale-like, don't you? I want life to be easy, happy and problem free. And it's not. I can sometimes wonder: Lord, do you see me?

Each week of our study, we are going to look briefly at the life a person in the Bible then connect our themes from Psalm 139 to their lives and ours. Let the Word of God sink into your mind and heart.

Let's pray that the Spirit of God connects their lives, His Word, His Truth and Gospel to our season of life—for change. Change in how we see and trust the Lord and change for how we see ourselves and others! Let's trust Him together!

This week we are going to look at Hagar. Do you remember her? She was definitely a small character in the book of Genesis, but seemingly a big pain in the life of Abraham and Sarah. You could say she was a problem.

Hagar was an Egyptian-born woman who was given to Abraham as a slave, a handmaiden to Sarah—and the mother of Abraham's son, Ishmael.

Honestly, I feel sorry for Hagar. She was a slave to circumstances, people, position, culture, and her feelings. I'm guessing that as a woman, she wasn't where she wanted to be, doing what she wanted to do...and she was certainly not free. Can you relate to any of those feelings? I can.

She became a woman filled with fear, anger, resentment, pride and the courage to run away. She was rejected and hopeless. She was not the chosen woman of God's covenantal promises, she didn't play a role in the big-picture redemptive plan of God at all, but God saw her. He initiated a conversation with her and spoke to her, twice.

Do you realize that she is the only woman recorded in the Bible that the Lord spoke to, twice? I find that simply astounding. Twice. She was a "nobody," by all human counts, yet God saw her. Genesis 16 is the first time where we see God by His name, "El Roi," the God who sees me. I think we get a little window into the heart of God through Hagar's life. God loves people. He is working in ways that we don't always understand. I have no idea how Hagar felt about her interactions with the Lord, but I think it's important to see that, even though her line was not going to be part of His covenantal plans, He valued her. He is a God who sees.

Check out Hagar's story in Genesis 16 and Genesis 21:9–19.

Seen by a Teen: *I find it so easy to want to run away from my issues and my feelings. It seems like such a good idea to "pack my bags" and run away from my messy life and "let it be." Issues like school obligations, confusing emotions, relationships and the unknown future. Sometimes I want to run away because I feel like I am alone and that I'm the only one who feels this way.*

Could you imagine what life would be like if everyone ran away from their problems? Nothing would get solved. There would be more hate and bitterness than there already is, and life would be miserable.

Imagine if the Lord ran away from us because we were too much of a mess. We would never have a chance for salvation and redemption from the mess. Unlike me, Hagar ran from her "problem," partly in fear and partly in anger, and during her fleeing the Lord sought her out and found her. He found her and spoke to her in her mess. He wanted her to know that He sees her. He sees.

If He saw her then, we can know He sees me and you. He doesn't always fix our messes, but He sees us in the midst and shows Himself faithful. That gives me comfort. Or at least it should…

The story of Hagar gives me comfort, too…or at least it should. My life hasn't been like Hagar's at all. Compared to her, mine has been a bed of roses! But, I have had seasons of tremendous fear, anger, resentment and hopelessness. Adult life has been a lot more challenging than I ever thought it would be! Following Jesus and trusting Him with my life and the lives of the people I love has been a lot more challenging than I thought it would be. Sometimes I have wanted out and emotionally I have run away, even from the Lord and yet He sees and knows. Let's connect with the Word.

Searching the Word: In your study time this week, make sure to pause and pray for the Holy Spirit to teach you. I'd encourage you to take the time to read each text from another version of the Bible, too. If you have the time, read the context around our verses of the week and look up any words you find interesting. Then, continue with marking words, making lists, or answering the questions that I ask in each of the following texts of the week. Enjoy this time. Dig in and let God's Word meet you! Read the following text and mark the words for God, including any pronouns (You, Your, LORD)

Psalm 139:1–5

"1 O LORD, You have searched me and known me.

2 You know when I sit down and when I rise up;

You understand my thought from afar.

3 You scrutinize my path and my lying down,

And are intimately acquainted with all my ways.

4 Even before there is a word on my tongue,

Behold, O LORD, You know it all.

5 You have enclosed me behind and before,

And laid Your hand upon me."

According to the text, what does the Lord do for you? I see about ten things. List what you see.

1.

2.

3.

4.

5.

6.

7.

8.

9.

10.

Look up the following words. You can look them up in a dictionary or Google search them. Type in the exact phrase and the Hebrew Strong's number and see what additional insights you find.

Known: (Hebrew Strong's number 3045)

Scrutinize: (Hebrew Strong's number 2219)

What did you learn?

Now, read the next section and mark the words I and me.

Psalm 139:6–9

"6 Such knowledge is too wonderful for me;

It is too high, I cannot attain to it.

7 Where can I go from Your Spirit?

Or where can I flee from Your presence?

8 If I ascend to heaven, You are there;

If I make my bed in Sheol, behold, You are there.

9 If I take the wings of the dawn,

If I dwell in the remotest part of the sea"

What is the psalmist's point? Where can we go to get away from God?

Where have you tried to hide from God? How have you tried to hide?

Have you ever had a time where you thought you were hidden from the Lord?

In the next section of text, mark every reference to God and to me.

Psalm 139:10–12

"10 Even there Your hand will lead me,

And Your right hand will lay hold of me.

11 If I say, "Surely the darkness will overwhelm me,

And the light around me will be night,"

12 Even the darkness is not dark to You,

And the night is as bright as the day.

Darkness and light are alike to You."

List what you learn about God and about yourself

God   I/me

What do you learn about darkness and light?

Seen by a Teen: *I was afraid of the dark as kid, but this isn't talking about literal darkness…it's talking about the tribulations of life. Now, I can tend to be afraid of the "darkness" of life, but I don't have to be. I'm a work in progress, I fear failing. I want to be perfect and not be considered a failure to myself or others. This can be a very dark place for me, but the Lord is faithfully leading from the "darkness" to His light. Because the Lord is greater than the darkness…it's all light to Him.*

What is a fear that you have that you can allow the Lord to give "light" to?

Look back over Psalm 139:1–12 and record what He is showing you about Himself. What hits your heart the most? What troubles you? Do you learn anything about yourself? Record your insights.

Let's look at a text in Isaiah about God's character. Read slowly and mark every reference to God and underline what He is doing.

Isaiah 40:12–14

"12 Who has measured the waters in the hollow of His hand,

And marked off the heavens by the span,

And calculated the dust of the earth by the measure,

And weighed the mountains in a balance

And the hills in a pair of scales?

13 Who has directed the Spirit of the LORD,

Or as His counselor has informed Him?

14 With whom did He consult and who gave Him understanding?

And who taught Him in the path of justice and taught Him knowledge

And informed Him of the way of understanding?"

List what the Lord is doing and can do.

Seen by a Teen: *I love how the text says, "Who can fathom the Spirit of the Lord?" (v. 13, NIV) I can't even begin to understand the full power and greatness of Him. It's crazy to think about the fact that the Lord has no beginning. He is. He wasn't taught. He didn't grow. He has always been at maximum power and glory.*

We grow up, we learn and age. Hopefully, not age like my mother but like my grandmother! (Just kidding.) We are constantly learning and growing, and we certainly don't do it perfectly! It's a sobering and comforting thought that we can put our life, trust and learning in the Lord God who never changes.

What are you seeing about our God? This God who sees and knows you! The next two texts look out to the nations and the universe, but remember: He still sees and knows you, too. Mark every reference to God and underline what He is comparing.

Isaiah 40:15–20

"15 Behold, the nations are like a drop from a bucket,

And are regarded as a speck of dust on the scales;

Behold, He lifts up the islands like fine dust.

16 Even Lebanon is not enough to burn,

Nor its beasts enough for a burnt offering.

17 All the nations are as nothing before Him,

They are regarded by Him as less than nothing and meaningless.

18 To whom then will you liken God?

Or what likeness will you compare with Him?

19 As for the idol, a craftsman casts it,

A goldsmith plates it with gold,

And a silversmith fashions chains of silver.

20 He who is too impoverished for such an offering

Selects a tree that does not rot;

He seeks out for himself a skillful craftsman

To prepare an idol that will not totter.'

What are some things we "worship" other than God? We don't generally "bow down" to literal idols, but what kind of idols do you "bow down" to, looking for help, hope and significance?

If I'm honest, I often "bow down" to myself and my desires. I definitely struggle with looking for my value and worth in the things I do and in the relationships I have, particularly as a wife, mom and ministry leader. I easily "worship" any and all of these things, and they all totter and fall don't they? They change. Circumstances, people and feelings constantly change, that is why they make terrible "gods." The Lord is the only One who does not change, and He knows it! Praise His name!

In the following text, once again mark every reference to God, including any pronouns, and underline all that He does. Slow down and take it in.

Isaiah 40:21–26

"21 Do you not know? Have you not heard?

Has it not been declared to you from the beginning?

Have you not understood from the foundations of the earth?

22 It is He who sits above the circle of the earth,

And its inhabitants are like grasshoppers,

Who stretches out the heavens like a curtain

And spreads them out like a tent to dwell in.

23 He it is who reduces rulers to nothing,

Who makes the judges of the earth meaningless.

24 Scarcely have they been planted,

Scarcely have they been sown,

Scarcely has their stock taken root in the earth,

But He merely blows on them, and they wither,

And the storm carries them away like stubble.

25 "To whom then will you liken Me

That I would be his equal?" says the Holy One.

26 Lift up your eyes on high

And see who has created these stars,

The One who leads forth their host by number,

He calls them all by name;

Because of the greatness of His might and the strength of His power,

Not one of them is missing."

Consider the authorities of this world and the people in our lives to whom we look for security...do we ever find lasting security? What do you learn about the Lord?

Go back and re-read Psalm 139:1–2 and Isaiah 40:26. Contrast the stars and you.

Stars   You

With a God this big, holding the universe, world, and nations together, does He miss out on seeing you? How does this hit your heart?

In the following text from Romans, mark every reference to God, including any pronouns. Then, underline the word and.

Romans 11:33–36

"33 Oh, the depth of the riches both of the wisdom and knowledge of God! How unsearchable are His judgments and unfathomable His ways! 34 For WHO HAS KNOWN THE MIND OF THE LORD, OR WHO BECAME HIS COUNSELOR? 35 Or WHO HAS FIRST GIVEN TO HIM THAT IT MIGHT BE PAID BACK TO HIM AGAIN? 36 For from Him and through Him and to Him are all things. To Him be the glory forever. Amen."

List what you learn about God from this text.

What words or concepts does the word "and" connect in this text.

Will we ever get to the end of knowing and understanding the wisdom and knowledge of God? Why or why not? What does this text teach you about eternity?

Seen by a Teen: *[Question: What is one thing that stood out to you in this week's lesson?]*

The Lord is the greatest romantic, not like the movies and gooey feelings of love, but true love. Agape love. Everything that He created has a design and unique structure and He loves His creation.

We read the verse in Matthew 10:30, "But the very hairs on your head are all numbered" and I think it is easy to take that too lightly. The Lord knows our names, the exact number of hairs on our heads, our fingerprints…and the thought of that brings me to tears. The Creator of the ends of the earth knows, sees and loves you and me.

Ponder: This is just a series of questions and comments to think on. I'm a big fan of thinking, so think with me!

We have a really big God, don't we? A God who knows, sees and is intimately acquainted with everything! Even you. How does that make you feel? Is that easy or hard for you to believe? Does that make you feel safe or troubled? Or a bit of both?

As you reflect on the life of Hagar and the texts of this week, what comes together for you? What is confusing? How can God be so big and awesome and yet know everything about us—and still care about us, too? Do you have an area of your life that you struggle to believe that He cares for you? Have you had other areas where you have known and experienced His care? Think about it. How does God's Word meet you in those situations?

He sees you and He knows you…and He has made a way for you to know Him. We are known in order to know Him and grow in knowing Him. Did you know that Jesus defined eternal life in John 17:3, as knowing God? "This is eternal life, that they may know You, the only true God, and Jesus Christ whom You have sent."

We are fully known by God in order that we may come to know Him through our faith and trust in Jesus Christ's life, death, burial and resurrection, which offers us the free gift of life. That life is a deep relationship of knowing Him. This is our God! What grace, what love! What hope in a dark world that desperately needs His Light.

Pulling Together: If you have time, read over the texts of the week one more time and consider the following questions:

• What do you learn about the character of God—Father, Son, and Spirit—in the texts of the week?

• Is there a thread of the hope of the Gospel in the text? Where do you see it?

• Is there a window into the human heart? What is it? What do you learn about yourself and about other people relative to you?

• Where do you need to stop, consider, pray, receive truth or walk in faith? Write down what He is showing you to do.

Keepsakes: Keep God's Word in your heart! This week write out Psalm 139:1 at least two times. Get it into your mind and heart!

Psalm 139:1, "O LORD, You have searched me and known me…"

Sharing Your Heart: Sharing your heart with the Lord in prayer or by journaling your thoughts is a great way to practice knowing and being known. Yes, He already knows, but processing with Him is a huge help! Take some time and use these prompts to process with Him.

Oh LORD, the truth that You know me so intimately, better than I know myself, make me feel…

Thank You LORD for…May You…

Reach Out: Pray about the people you interact with this week and ask the Lord to show you someone that may be feeling alone and isolated. Ask the Lord to show you what you could do or say to come alongside them to let them know that He sees them? Then, do it!

Week one is done! We have a God who sees and knows you! Not just in general, but very specifically. He knows us better than we know ourselves. He sees our real needs. Next week, we'll get into that truth. Thank you for joining us. It's a joy to dig into the Word with you. We have prayed for you and we're trusting the Lord will work His Word into your life. You are loved!

?

Week 1: Notes

Week 2:

You...On Purpose

For the next two weeks, we'll look at the life and faith journey of the Apostle Peter. I love Peter. He was full of flaws, just like all of us, but he had a heart that desired to know Jesus. Walking with Jesus, Peter was at the beginning stages of faith. He had a lot of "faith" in himself but he didn't realize it. Jesus knew this about Peter and He chose him anyway. I think that is amazingly cool. He chose Peter on purpose. He knew who Peter was going to be, just as He knows you and me. Peter's "little faith" eventually grew into mature faith, but it was a long process and filled with failure.

I love that the Lord isn't in a rush. I love the grace and patience of His maturing process, although I'm not always a fan of my failures! Yet, even those failures have a work to do in us.

This week we'll look at few places in Peter's faith journey. Keep in mind what Jesus knew. He knew Peter through and through. He knew who Peter would become. He also knew Peter needed what only He could provide: salvation from his slavery to sin and self. Peter needed the life, death, burial and resurrection of Jesus in order to be brought into the Body of Christ, sealed with the power source of the Holy Spirit, as his part. Read the following texts and remember these events really took place: these are real people in a real place and time!

Luke 5:1–11

Matthew 14:22–33

Matthew 16:13–23

Seen by a Teen: *Like Peter, I think I have faith, but sometimes it is so hard to comprehend what the Lord has done and is doing. It's so easy to lose sight that He is the One who can and does do everything. Just like Peter, when he was walking on the water and lost sight of Jesus because of the waves and the wind, I tend to lose sight of Jesus when I'm called out of my comfort zone at school. Whether it is to love unlovable people or speak the truth in love, I can get distracted by my feelings and lose sight of the Lord.*

Don't you love it? Peter gets these awesome glimpses of who Jesus is: God! He also gets glimpses of who he himself is: afraid, lacking in faith, on the wrong page, and yet not disqualified. As you study the texts of the week, remember that the Lord knows you, and you are you...on purpose!

Searching the Word: In your study time this week, make sure to pause and pray for the Holy Spirit to teach you. I'd encourage you to take the time to read each text from another version of the Bible, too. If you have the time, read the context around our verses of the week and look up any words you find interesting. Then, continue with marking words, making lists, or answering the questions that I ask in each of the following texts of the week. Enjoy this time. Dig in and let God's Word meet you! As you read, slow down and mark each reference to God (including pronouns) and I, my, and me.

Psalm 139:13—18

"13 For You formed my inward parts;

You wove me in my mother's womb.

14 I will give thanks to You, for I am fearfully and wonderfully made;

Wonderful are Your works,

And my soul knows it very well.

15 My frame was not hidden from You,

When I was made in secret,

And skillfully wrought in the depths of the earth;

16 Your eyes have seen my unformed substance;

And in Your book were all written

The days that were ordained for me,

When as yet there was not one of them.

17 How precious also are Your thoughts to me, O God!

How vast is the sum of them!

18 If I should count them, they would outnumber the sand.

When I awake, I am still with You."

What verbs are used of God's work in making you? List them.

How are you described?

Pick out at least one of the verbs used to describe how God made you and look it up in a dictionary. Record your insights. Why did that particular word connect with you?

Read the verses one more time. How does this make you feel? Is this hard for you to believe?

Seen by a Teen: *I don't know about you, but some days, I can barely remember what I had for breakfast…so think about these verses, the Lord has millions of thoughts and never forgets a single one. As humans, we struggle to remember things in our everyday life: our to-do lists and appointments, and it can make us not very reliable. We tend to forget and then we end up having to ask for forgiveness for forgetting! God never forgets His thoughts of you: "Oh Lord, I'll never be able to comprehend them." Since the day that we were born, He has had thoughts of you and of me. Billons of people on this earth…and He still remembers you.*

There is no one like you. You are unique. You are on purpose. You are you.

Now, as sweet and wonderful as babies are…they grow up, don't they? And, it doesn't take very long to notice that we don't have to give any private lessons to toddlers on how to lie, cheat or steal, do we? We all know how to do that naturally!

Genesis 3 tells us that when sin entered the world, it gave humanity an unfixable problem. The problem of sin. We are born broken. The promise in the garden of Eden still stands: there will be a Seed (Genesis 3:15) who will crush the head of the enemy of our souls (satan). Jesus will conquer sin.

Jesus was the Lamb of God who willingly laid down His perfect unblemished life as a sacrifice for sin. The wrath, justice and punishment of sin fell upon Him who knew no sin (2 Corinthians 5:21) and He died in our place. He was buried. He rose again. Because He had no sin of His own to pay, He paid ours in our place!

The Father looked at the sacrifice (His perfect faith-filled life of obedience under the law of God, fulfilling the law, and His perfect death taking on the judgment of the law) and was satisfied (Isaiah 53:11), and the same Spirit that raised Jesus (Romans 8:11) now offers us true eternal life in Him, by grace and through faith in the finished work of Jesus Christ (Ephesians 1:13–14 and Ephesians 2:8–10).

This is why Jesus came. He didn't come to simply be an example to follow…we needed much more than that! He came to give life itself. Life to dead people! He truly sees who we are. He sees our true need. We need Him.

Do we see what He sees? You…He knows you and who you are to become in Him! Have you placed your faith in Him alone to rescue you from sin?

In the following verses from Matthew, mark every reference to Christ including pronouns.

Matthew 9:35–38

"35 Jesus was going through all the cities and villages, teaching in their synagogues and proclaiming the gospel of the kingdom, and healing every kind of disease and every kind of sickness.

36 Seeing the people, He felt compassion for them, because they were distressed and dispirited like sheep without a shepherd. 37 Then He said to His disciples, "The harvest is plentiful, but the workers are few. 38 Therefore beseech the Lord of the harvest to send out workers into His harvest."

What did Jesus do?

Take a few minutes and look up two words:

Seeing (Greek Strong's number 1492)

Dispirited (Greek Strong's number 4496)

What do you learn? What did Jesus actually see?

Was the people's biggest problem physical or spiritual? Where do we tend to believe our biggest problems are?

What did Jesus feel for them? Why?

Whose harvest is it?

He knew them all, as they were being formed in their mothers' wombs. What does this tell you about Jesus?

Seen by a Teen: *I have a certain "quality" called people-pleasing. It's naturally woven into me. Trust me, it's not always a gift. It can be a problem because I tend to want to "please" and "fix" people. I'm learning that it's Jesus' job to fix people. When I read about Jesus looking over the confused and aimless crowd, the first thought that came to my mind was that I would be freaking out. I would want to help, and I'm only human, and I can only do so much. Everything in me wants to fix people's problems and save them, but I wasn't the one created to do that.*

Jesus had no sin, Jesus was not a people-pleaser but a God-pleaser. He had God's love for people and knew that He alone could handle the brokenness of people.

As much as I would love to heal diseased bodies, sadly I was not given that gift, and honestly if I saw all that need I would want to run away. Jesus saw, knew and didn't run. Instead, He said, "What a huge harvest! How few workers there are, so get on your knees and pray for more harvest hands." I want to learn how to be His harvest hand, do you?

What is hitting your heart?

Jesus didn't come to set the angels free. He didn't come to redeem the trees or the animals. He came to redeem people. He loves people—broken image-bearers of God. That is whom He loves so much He laid down His life. For you. God formed you and, if you are in Christ, He is forming you into the image of His Son. If you are not in Christ, He is calling you by name to, "Come. Come."

Read this text from Hebrews slowly and mark every reference to Jesus, including any pronouns.

Hebrews 2:14–16

"14 Therefore, since the children share in flesh and blood, He Himself likewise also partook of the same, that through death He might render powerless him who had the power of death, that is, the devil, 15 and might free those who through fear of death were subject to slavery all their lives. 16 For assuredly He does not give help to angels, but He gives help to the descendant of Abraham."

What were we in slavery to?

What does this text tell you about the value of humanity to God?

What did it "cost" Jesus?

Again, mark every reference to Christ including pronouns.

Hebrews 2:17–18

"17 Therefore, He had to be made like His brethren in all things, so that He might become a merciful and faithful high priest in things pertaining to God, to make propitiation for the sins of the people. 18 For since He Himself was tempted in that which He has suffered, He is able to come to the aid of those who are tempted."

What "job" does Jesus hold? How does He do this job?

Can He understand our temptations? Why?

Propitiation is a very interesting word. It means reconciliation and atonement, but there is something very specific about this word at its root. There is removal of the sin.

Jesus did not simply put aside sin or cover it over; He took it away. His sacrifice satisfied the debt of sin , for the purpose of removing it. For good. As far as the east is from the west, our sin, in Christ Jesus, has been removed. Never to be brought up again. He knows it all. He hasn't forgotten, He has removed it. Wow.

I hope you are seeing the thread here. He sees us, the true us, and doesn't leave us in the mess that we are in. He came to redeem us and bring us into a new creation He is making: His Body and Bride!

Read the following verses in Ephesians. Look for the past tense words and mark them. Paul is writing to those who have trusted in Christ, and he is reminding them of who they used to be outside of Christ.

Ephesians 2:1–3

"1 And you were dead in your trespasses and sins, 2 in which you formerly walked according to the course of this world, according to the prince of the power of the air, of the spirit that is now working in the sons of disobedience. 3 Among them we too all formerly lived in the lusts of our flesh, indulging the desires of the flesh and of the mind, and were by nature children of wrath, even as the rest."

List at least five things that we were outside of Christ. Formerly we....

1.

2.

3.

4.

5.

Have you ever considered that this was your position outside of Christ? I didn't for a very long time! I was a "good girl." I was religious. I tried very hard to obey the rules and my parents. I worked hard at being good and, when I compared myself to a lot of other people, I was! I had no idea that my "good" wasn't good enough.

I had no idea these verses look very different on every single person. My "deadness" looked like a pretty "corpse," but dead is dead. Only Jesus, not my good works, could make me alive! I harshly judged those "really ugly dead people," and had no idea that I was just as dead.

Seen by a Teen: *In The Message version of the Bible it says that when we were still in spiritual darkness and unsaved, "we let the world, which doesn't know the first thing about living, tell us how to live" (Eph. 2:2).*

Everyone grows up this way, there's no escaping it until you put your trust in Christ and are born into a new way of living. Learning this new way of living, though, is not fast or easy. Socially, we are living in this world and there is constant pressure to look and act like the world. Just like Peter, once again, we get flooded by the world's expectations and it is so easy to lose sight of the Lord.

But God. Two of the most powerful verses in the New Testament. But God. If not for Him we would be completely lost. From before the foundation of the earth, God had an eternal plan in Christ Jesus.

In the following verses, underline the phrase But God, then mark every reference to Christ, including all pronouns.

Ephesians 2:4–7

"4 But God, being rich in mercy, because of His great love with which He loved us, 5 even when we were dead in our transgressions, made us alive together with Christ (by grace you have been saved), 6 and raised us up with Him, and seated us with Him in the heavenly places in Christ Jesus, 7 so that in the ages to come He might show the surpassing riches of His grace in kindness toward us in Christ Jesus."

What did God, in Christ Jesus, do for us? When? Why?

Go back and mark the phrase in Christ and the pronouns you and we.

Now, look up the word Workmanship (Greek Strong's number 4161)

Ephesians 2:8–10

" 8 For by grace you have been saved through faith; and that not of yourselves, it is the gift of God; 9 not as a result of works, so that no one may boast. 10 For we are His workmanship, created in Christ Jesus for good works, which God prepared beforehand so that we would walk in them."

How are we saved? Why?

We are saved from our deadness in sin but what are saved to?

How many workmanships are there? Is it singular? What does the text say?

What does it mean to be your part of His workmanship? How personal and detailed do you think His workmanship is? If you are in Christ Jesus, you are a specific part of His workmanship. How does that strike you?

Seen by a Teen: *At 15 years of age, how does it feel to know that Jesus knows you intimately, better than you know yourself, and knows who you can become?*

It's a big fat relief. It's such a comfort because the Lord knows me better than I know myself; I don't even know me! The way that I picture God in my relationship with Him is literally like He is cradling me in His arms. He's constantly holding me and guiding me—what is there to fear in that?

Not fleshly fear, like fear of the dark, but spiritual fear...there's no need for spiritual fear. But, that is still a constant struggle for me. It looks different on all of us.

Since the day that He created the heavens and the earth He knew my name. He knew how many hairs I would have on my head and when I'd be born. He knew that about you, too. It's crazy. When you want to run away from your issues, the Lord is seeking you. He's not looking to judge you He's looking to lead and shape you and me.

Ponder: How does it feel to be so thoroughly known by the Lord from your conception? Do you ever struggle thinking He made a mistake? I have! There are plenty of things that I have wished were different about me—some physical, some mental, some emotional, and even some things about my personality.

Why can't I be more...

Or

Why do I think and react like...

Or

Why am I so...

How about you? I'm an overthinker. I'm a verbal processor. I'm a highly responsible person. I feel things deeply. I see hurts and wounds in others and want to help. All of these things are hardwired into me and, there are times I've wished all of them weren't me!

Left to my own natural wiring I can get myself into a lot of trouble. But, as the Lord faithfully shows me how to follow Him and be Spirit-led and Spirit-directed in my wiring, it can be very encouraging, helpful, and rewarding as my part of His workmanship.

Does that make any sense? He made each of us well. He knew what He was doing. But, we need Him in order to be who He has made us to be. We need to be led by Him! He knows how to shape His nature into us; He knows how to infuse life, faith and His likeness into the people He created us to be.

What about you? What do you love and what do you dislike about how He has made you? Do you see the value of your part? Can you accept the beauty of His sacrifice to buy you back and bring you into His masterpiece as your part? How does this help you see others? What is stirring in your heart?

You…are you on purpose!

Pulling Together: If you have time, read over the texts of the week one more time and consider the following questions:

- What do you learn about the character of God—Father, Son, and Spirit—in the texts of the week?

- Is there a thread of the hope of the Gospel in the text? Where do you see it?

- Is there a window into the human heart? What is it? What do you learn about yourself and about other people relative to you?

- Where do you need to stop, consider, pray, receive truth or walk in faith? Write down what He is showing you to do.

Keepsakes: This week were going to keep Psalm 139:13 in our hearts. Write out the verse at least two times and treasure it. You are treasured!

Psalm 139:13, "You formed my inward parts; You wove me together in my mother's womb…"

Sharing Your Heart: Use these prompts to spend some time with the Lord sharing your heart…

Deep down my soul knows…. even though I don't always feel… You are….

What do You see when You see me, Lord? Show me….

Reach Out: Think and pray about some things that you are unclear on about yourself, whether it is an emotional wound or something you struggle with. Or possibly understanding your spiritual gifting. Then, write down what the Lord shows you. Find someone you know who is struggling with the same thing and share what He showed you or use your gifting to encourage them.

Week 2: Notes

Week 3:

The problem with us all...

The problem with us all is that we see what we see. We oftentimes judge only by what we can see, don't we? I tend to see things from my earthly perspective and oftentimes feel like things are not fair.

Take this writing time for example. As I told you, Maggie and I were snowed into a sweet little bungalow writing this study. This place was an absolute gift from the Lord. Warm, beautiful, quiet. We had a great time together preparing and writing. It was special.

Towards the end of our time away, though, Maggie went home. I was staying for another day or so, but I decided to tidy up and prepared to forge out for the first time in three days. We had 18 inches of snow dropped on us, my car was covered, and I was literally snowed into the driveway.

Feeling proud of myself, I used my "break time" to stretch my muscles with a little "light" shoveling (can you hear my sarcasm?) I trudged out for what I thought was only going to be a few minutes.

Coat? Check.

Gloves? Check.

Jeans? Check. (I didn't want to horrify the neighbors in my pajama pants!)

Shovel? Check.

Phone? Nah. Let's go!

Click. The door shut.

Yep. You guessed it. I locked myself out!

Three hours later...I will repeat...THREE HOURS of "light" shoveling, getting soaking wet while searching for a hidden key, freezing in the cold, enlisting the help of two wonderfully gracious friends, and wanting to just drop in a snow bank and cry angry tears.

I wondered why this was happening. I thought "This isn't fair!" I was doing a good thing there! I had had a sweet time of fellowship with the Lord, the Word, Maggie and my computer. WHY?!

How could I go from having a calm, sweet, devoted spirit, to being a cold, angry mess? Because I'm me, and that cold angry mess lives in me. I just don't see it; I see what I want to see.

I think Peter was the same. He genuinely thought he had enough love to love and follow Jesus wherever He led. As we will see today, though, he didn't. We need God's Spirit for everything. When Jesus said in John 15:5, "Apart from Me, you can do nothing..." He actually meant that.

We can't genuinely love, follow, obey or be filled with joy without Christ and His Spirit. We need Jesus for everything!

I get trapped with my focus on my circumstances, myself, other people and my feelings! But, God's grace meets me there, to show me myself and to show me my need. To show me the hot/cold angry mess of my heart and my need to cling to Him.

Take a look at these texts about Peter and imagine his emotions. Peter had the "want" to follow Jesus to the end, but he didn't have the "how" to follow him...yet. How do we follow Jesus? By the power of the Holy Spirit. Step by step. Day by day. Moment by moment...growing us up in faith.

John 13:34–38

Matthew 26:69–75

John 21:15–22

Seen by a Teen: *We all see what we see and it's not always God's perspective. As I look back, at the time of my grandpa's Alzheimers, I can honestly say I don't understand what God was doing. It was a time of fear, confusion, and hurt and I didn't know, at the time, what the Lord was going to do with it. I could only see the circumstances.*

I still don't see it all, but I'm seeing how the Lord is exposing some deep wounds in me that need healing. Somehow, I know that the Lord is going to use the struggles for His purposes. That gives me hope, because He can use struggles and wounds instead of just letting them stay.

Have you ever had a wound that was too painful to touch? I had an ingrown toenail once. It was awful. I couldn't walk. I couldn't wear a shoe. It got infected. I soaked it. I put medicine on it and bandaged it. I tried everything, and nothing worked. It only got worse. Finally, I went to the doctor. I didn't want him to touch it, but he had to. He had to cut it out. He had to open it up, get the infection out, get the nail out, medicate it and bandage it. In order to save my toe, more pain was inflicted.

Our hearts are wounded with sin wounds. Sometimes it's from personal sin or another's sin, sometimes it's simply from living in a sin-cursed world. Sin, pain, wounds, infection—it all hurts. But, often, for there to be salvation, healing, and wholeness, more pain is required to get the infection and the problem out.

The Lord does not expose sin because He likes to cause pain but because it's the only way we can heal deep down. Do I always believe that? Or do I just get angry and ask why?

Peter needed to see himself. He needed to get to the end of self-reliance—and so do I. Until the day we see Jesus, either by our death or when He comes back, we are called to walk the road of "decreasing" our self-reliance and "increasing" our trust and reliance in the Lord. His ways are not always our ways, but He is in the business of healing heart wounds.

Searching the Word: In your study time this week, make sure to pause and pray for the Holy Spirit to teach you. I'd encourage you to take the time to read each text from another version of the Bible, too. If you have the time, read the context around our verses of the week and look up any words you find interesting. Then, continue with marking words, making lists, or answering the questions that I ask in each of the following texts of the week. Enjoy this time. Dig in and let God's Word meet you!

In the following two texts, mark the words I, me, and my.

Psalm 139:19—22

"19 O that You would slay the wicked, O God;

Depart from me, therefore, men of bloodshed.2

0 For they speak against You wickedly,

And Your enemies take Your name in vain.

21 Do I not hate those who hate You, O LORD?

And do I not loathe those who rise up against You?

22 I hate them with the utmost hatred;

They have become my enemies."

Isaiah 40:27

"27 Why do you say, O Jacob, and assert, O Israel,

"My way is hidden from the Lord,

And the justice due me escapes the notice of my God"?

What did you learn by marking I, me, and my?

The text from Psalms is more introspective and the text from Isaiah is focused towards God. What do you see about the authors perspective?

Which do you see: justification, anger, disappointment, self-righteousness? What else?

We all see what we see, but God sees things differently doesn't He? He sees everything far deeper.

Mark the references to God, including the pronouns, in the following verses.

Isaiah 55:8–9

8 "For My thoughts are not your thoughts,

Nor are your ways My ways," declares the Lord.

9 "For as the heavens are higher than the earth,

So are My ways higher than your ways

And My thoughts than your thoughts."

What do you learn about God?

How are God's ways different than ours?

Seen by a Teen: *Thank goodness the Lord doesn't think or work the that way I do, because I have a crazy way of working and thinking! I'm also thankful that He doesn't work and think like my mom, she's crazy too! The Lord has a very specific and intricate plan and I certainly don't understand it all, but He does. Everything that has ever been created is tied to something else. Ultimately, He has a great plan.*

Mark all the references to God and any pronouns in these verses from Isaiah. Look for the water cycle in this text.

Isaiah 55:10–11

"10 For as the rain and the snow come down from heaven,

And do not return there without watering the earth

And making it bear and sprout,

And furnishing seed to the sower and bread to the eater;

11 So will My word be which goes forth from My mouth;

It will not return to Me empty,

Without accomplishing what I desire,

And without succeeding in the matter for which I sent it."

What do you learn about the Lord?

Why is the water cycle used as an example? What do you learn in connection to God's ways and Word?

In the next verses, mark the word and.

Isaiah 55:12–13

12 "For you will go out with joy

And be led forth with peace;

The mountains and the hills will break forth into shouts of joy before you,

And all the trees of the field will clap their hands.

13 "Instead of the thorn bush the cypress will come up,

And instead of the nettle the myrtle will come up,

And it will be a memorial to the Lord,

For an everlasting sign which will not be cut off."

And is a connector word. Write out what and connects in the text and consider how God's ways are different than ours .

What do you learn?

Verse 13 is an amazing verse. In the original Hebrew text this verse indicates the "transformation of the desert." Re-read Isaiah 55:8–13 and think about all the concepts. Pull them together. Why, how, and for what purpose does God transform a desert-like existence to lush, productive and fruitful existence?

What do you learn about the Lord and His ways?

Mark the references to God including any pronouns in the following text.

Isaiah 40:28–29

"28 Do you not know? Have you not heard?

The Everlasting God, the Lord, the Creator of the ends of the earth

Does not become weary or tired. His understanding is inscrutable.

29 He gives strength to the weary,

And to him who lacks might He increases power."

What are the names of God used?

He never gets…

What is the Lord able to do?

Seen by a Teen: *Right now, I need some fresh strength because I'm tired and weary. I'm complaining about how I need more strength and God never sleeps, never gets thirsty or hungry. He doesn't get weary and He is constantly dealing with everyone!*

That is crazy good. Thank goodness! If I was God, I would have a secretary that would constantly say, "I'm sorry she's not in right now…she is taking her third nap of the day," or "She's busy eating her fourth lunch!"

The Lord never gets weary or tired out. He doesn't fail. He calls us to come to Him for our energy, strength and rejuvenation. Thank the Lord He is who He says He is!

In the next text, mark the words though, those, and they.

Isaiah 40:30–31

"30 Though youths grow weary and tired,

And vigorous young men stumble badly,

31 Yet those who wait for the Lord

Will gain new strength;

They will mount up with wings like eagles,

They will run and not get tired,

They will walk and not become weary."

What will always happen to us?

Where is the hope?

Look up the word for wait, Hebrew Strong's number 6960. What do you learn?

Re-read Isaiah 40:28–31. Is he talking about physical strength or something else? Why do you need to know this?

In this last text, Jesus is speaking. Mark the words I, me, and my.

Matthew 11:28–31

" 28 Come to Me, all who are weary and heavy-laden, and I will give you rest. 29 Take My yoke upon you and learn from Me, for I am gentle and humble in heart, and you will find rest for your souls. 30 For My yoke is easy and My burden is light."

Who is called to come to Him? Why?

Does Jesus only call the strong? What do you learn about the need to be weak and tired out?

What does this teach you about God's ways?

When we are tired, weary, and burdened and we humble ourselves and come, what will we find?

What are the instructions of Jesus?

Is this difficult for you? It is for me. I value strength. I value independence. I value not needing. Can you see why my own self-evaluation is flawed? What about you?

Seen by a Teen: *I can't handle much. I'm a lightweight. I'm thankful for Jesus who promised to carry my burdens for me. This is a good reminder that I don't have to carry everything by myself, that I'm actually called to put my issues/burdens into the Lord's hands. He wants me to find rest in Him because He knows that I can't do it on my own, even though I try sometimes. There's so much freedom in that. I was created to be loved and to love others and I can't do that if I'm trying to carry a million problems on my own.*

Ponder: What is hitting your heart this week? Do you see the threads? Peter's life of determination, self-evaluation of strength and ability, and then the truth of his failure (though not his disqualification.) The Lord qualifies the disqualified.

David, in his Psalm, looks at the "enemy" and sees himself as different, as better in his estimation. His last two verses are SO important! We'll see them next week.

Our ways and God's ways? Very different. Our perspective and the Lord's? Very, very different.

In Isaiah, the people ask why? Where are you God? This isn't fair! And, He replies with grace and truth. "I never get tired or weary, come to me." Jesus offers up a similar invitation. From a spiritual perspective, getting tired and weary is a good thing, because it's another level of coming to the end of ourselves.

Do you think that way? Do you want to be without strength in yourself? Do you look at the painful times when wounds are exposed as a gift of grace to show you your need for Him?

Do you get impatient with the process? Do you dislike the process, at times, as much as I do? But, are you learning to ask for His eyes to see a deeper and better work happening?

Are you running to Him? Coming, waiting, growing in faith and hope. Do you know He sees, knows and loves you in your mess? Even in the messy process?

How does all of this make you feel? Where are your eyes of faith?

Seen by a *Teen* [*Question: At 15, still growing in understanding yourself, the world and God's ways, what is one encouragement you could give other teens about God's perspective on life?*]

There's a lot of hope. The Lord doesn't give up. It's been all this time and He hasn't given up yet...He sent Jesus. The Lord stays true to Himself. Grow in relying on Him.

Pulling Together: If you have time, read over the texts of the week one more time and consider

the following questions:

•   What do you learn about the character of God—Father, Son, and Spirit—in the texts of the week?

•   Is there a thread of the hope of the Gospel in the text? Where do you see it?

- Is there a window into the human heart? What is it? What do you learn about yourself and about other people relative to you?

- Where do you need to stop, consider, pray, receive Truth or walk in faith? Write down what He is showing you to do.

Keepsakes: How have the verse been going for you? Are you "keeping" them in your heart? Write out the verse of the week at least two times.

Psalm 139:23, "Search me, O God, and know my heart; Try me and know my anxious thoughts…"

Sharing Your Heart: Is it hard for you to share your heart with the Lord or is it easy? I have a lot of opinions I like to give Him. I'm really thankful He understand me better than I understand myself. He is faithful to show me where I'm off. How about you? Spend some time with Him.

How do the truths of this week apply to me, Lord? Show me…

Lord, I acknowledge that my ways and Your ways are very different, Help me…

Thank you, Lord for….

Reach Out: Find a rock and write on it a burden that you have been struggling with, something that you need to lay down. Then, take the rock and throw it as far as you can into a river, pond…or even the garbage if you need to. Remember He has already carried it for you.

Notes: Week 3

Week 4:

Search me...

Can you believe this is our last week together? We hope and pray that the Lord is meeting you in His Word and with His Truth. I thought it was only fitting to take a look at the life of David in our final week and make some observations. Let's dive in!

David is best known for being "a man after God's own heart." Take a look at 1 Samuel 13:1–13, when David is anointed.

Imagine. A lot happens over the course of about 15 years. David kills Goliath. He becomes a mighty man of war serving under King Saul. He is popular. He is hunted down and on the run for years at the command of King Saul. Drama, drama, drama! Finally, David is crowned the King of Israel. He has seen the Lord's faithfulness. He has a heart for the LORD God and His people. He has penned many Psalms, beautiful Psalms filled with ranging emotions. It's probable that Psalm 139 is penned after his ascension as King.

Read Psalm 139 and see his heart, and then focus on the last two verses.

Search me...

I have loved Psalm 139 for many years, and I always thought that verses 19-22 were odd, the whole "do I not hate those who hate you, O LORD" section? Until I understand them in context, verses 19–22 are self-evaluation. He has searched himself and evaluates that he is on God's side.

The significance of verses 23–24 is David asking the LORD to search him, know him, lead in from any way of error, anything that he doesn't see. It's a humble request for the Lord's evaluation and it's beautiful. The Lord already knows, but David is asking to know too and be lead away from anything that is hurtful or harmful to the name of the LORD. It's submission.

Here's the thing though, for David and for us...it needs to be repeated. Over and over and over again until the day when our faith is made sight. This is about a living relationship of faith. Keep searching, keep knowing, keep trying these anxious thoughts and keep showing me any hurtful way in me; keep leading me in the everlasting way. Keep me keeping on with You.

Look at what happened after this Psalm was written. We can all lose our focus on the Lord and our eyes of faith can turn towards ourselves and what we want.

Read 2 Samuel 11:1—12:13

Yet, God didn't cast David away—even then. God searched him and showed David himself.

Seen by a Teen: *Anything can happen. Whether you are a believer or not, we are all capable doing things that we never thought we could do. David is the perfect example of this. There are always consequences to our sinful behavior, whether it's taking an extra cookie from the cookie jar or cheating on a test...what comes from that can be greater than the actual wrong doing. What if we got away with sin, from cheating on a test? Wouldn't we just keep it up?*

The more we sin and get away with it, the more we tend to do it...and the consequences only get greater. Sometimes the consequences are for us, but they can also spill over to others. David was in so much fear of being found out that sin piled onto more sin until it was a complete mess. What I see though, is redemption—even in the consequences. It's scary to think that we are all prone to sin, but I'm thankful we can be saved from it and not remain in it.

Searching the Word: In your study time this week, make sure to pause and pray for the Holy Spirit to teach you. I'd encourage you to take the time to read each text from another version of the Bible, too. If you have the time, read the context around our verses of the week and look up any words you find interesting. Then, continue with marking words, making lists, or answering the questions that I ask in each of the following texts of the week. Enjoy this time. Dig in and let God's Word meet you! In these final verses of Psalm 139, mark all references to God, including any pronouns.

Psalm 139:23—24

"23 Search me, O God, and know my heart;

Try me and know my anxious thoughts;

24 And see if there be any hurtful way in me,

And lead me in the everlasting way."

Look up two words:

Search (Hebrews Strong's number 2713)

Hurtful (Hebrew Strong's number 6090)

What six things does David ask God to do?

1.

2.

3.

4.

5.

6.

Think through the whole Psalm. God already knows David's request. What is the value of David asking God? Why ask God to do what He is already doing? How does this affect his relationship with God and others?

Seen by a Teen: *We know that God seeks us and knows us no matter what. But, it gives us so much more freedom when we ask the Lord to search our hearts, know our thoughts, and investigate our lives, because the Lord is already doing that.*

As we open up, we develop more trust and understanding with Lord. It becomes more and more of a two-way relationship of trust. We start welcoming Him into the mess of our hearts and minds instead of pushing Him away and closing off from Him.

Sometimes I wish that God didn't know everything about me because it's easy to close myself off and not look at the mess in me. I do that with people sometimes, but I can't do it with God. If we don't allow anyone in, especially Him, how will we heal and grow?

The Lord is in the business of exposing our areas of unbelief in Him, isn't He? Again, not to shame, hurt or humiliate us, but to heal and to increase our faith so that we find the wholeness, value, love, and significance we long for. This is a deep, lifelong work!

Read these verses from Hebrews and mark the word and.

Hebrews 4:12–13

"12 For the word of God is living and active and sharper than any two-edged sword, and piercing as far as the division of soul and spirit, of both joints and marrow, and able to judge the thoughts and intentions of the heart. 13 And there is no creature hidden from His sight, but all things are open and laid bare to the eyes of Him with whom we have to do."

There are 10 things connected by AND regarding the word of God; what are they?

1.   6.

2.   7.

3.   8.

4.   9.

5.   10

How deep does God's Word, His searching of our lives go?

How does that make you feel? Exposed? Comforted? Afraid?

Mark the word therefore and any reference to Christ in the following verses.

Hebrews 4:14–16

"14 Therefore, since we have a great high priest who has passed through the heavens, Jesus the Son of God, let us hold fast our confession. 15 For we do not have a high priest who cannot sympathize with our weaknesses, but One who has been tempted in all things as we are, yet without sin. 16 Therefore let us draw near with confidence to the throne of grace, so that we may receive mercy and find grace to help in time of need."

Who do we have when we are tempted?

What kind of high priest is He?

Why is this significant?

Look up the word confidence (Greek Strong's number 3326).

What two things are we called to do in this text?

1.

2.

What will we receive when we draw near, through Christ, to the throne room of God?

Now, pull the thoughts together. As brokenness, sin, unbelief is exposed in us by the Word and by God's ways, what are we to do? Run away? Try to fix it ourselves? Hide it?

Should we be afraid of asking the Lord to "search me and show me" what is hurtful in me? But do we fear being shown? Why?

How does this text help you?

Seen by a Teen: *I have a hard time not eating that second cookie my mom says I can't have. Jesus was tempted in every way possible and still trusted and obeyed God—He remained sinless. He also understands our temptations. Even cookie stealing.*

I have a hard time feeling like I'm all alone in my temptations sometimes. I know that it isn't true, but to think that Jesus not only struggled and won over temptation and He also dealt with a million more temptations...that's crazy to think about.

Not only is that a great testimony, but it is also a great encouragement to struggle against temptation, even though I oftentimes fall. I'm thankful that Jesus understands and is there to offer forgiveness. Not only can Jesus sympathize but He can also empathize, and He offers grace and mercy to help in our time of need.

Sadly, since He overcame every temptation I can't justify taking an extra cookie…even though I want to.

How is this coming together for you? The next text we are looking at deals with the two worlds in which we live: this temporary world and His eternal kingdom. We wake up every day in this temporary world in an "outer man/outer woman" shell, but with a new creation (the Holy Spirit) dwelling inside this "jar of clay."

When my eyes of faith, trust, and hope are on the things of this world and myself, I can get pretty overwhelmed, afraid and tired out. How about you? I can lose heart. I need to ask the Lord to "search me" and show me where my faith is misplaced. Learning to walk by faith and not by sight doesn't happen quickly or easily. Take a look!

Read the following texts and answer the following questions.

2 Corinthians 4:16

"16 Therefore we do not lose heart, but though our outer man is decaying, yet our inner man is being renewed day by day."

What is decaying, and which world does it belong to?

Who is being renewed and which world does it belong to?

Mark the word but in the following verses.

2 Corinthians 4:17–18

"17 For momentary, light affliction is producing for us an eternal weight of glory far beyond all comparison, 18 while we look not at the things which are seen, but at the things which are not seen; for the things which are seen are temporal, but the things which are not seen are eternal."

The two worlds are being contrasted. What is the contrast?

Seen   Unseen

Where are the afflictions?

What are they producing?

If our eyes of faith are only on what we see, do those afflictions produce as much? Why or why not?

In this next text, mark the words tent, house, building, dwelling, and home.

2 Corinthians 5:1–4

"5For we know that if the earthly tent which is our house is torn down, we have a building from God, a house not made with hands, eternal in the heavens. 2 For indeed in this house we groan, longing to be clothed with our dwelling from heaven, 3 inasmuch as we, having put it on, will not be found naked. 4 For indeed while we are in this tent, we groan, being burdened, because we do not want to be unclothed but to be clothed, so that what is mortal will be swallowed up by life. 5 Now He who prepared us for this very purpose is God, who gave to us the Spirit as a pledge. 6 Therefore, being always of good courage, and knowing that while we are at home in the body we are absent from the Lord— 7 for we walk by faith, not by sight— 8 we are of good courage, I say, and prefer rather to be absent from the body and to be at home with the Lord. 9 Therefore we also have as our ambition, whether at home or absent, to be pleasing to Him. 10 For we must all appear before the judgment seat of Christ, so that each one may be recompensed for his deeds in the body, according to what he has done, whether good or bad."

I understand that this is a wordy section of Scripture. But, slow down and look at the two worlds with two different "houses." This includes our bodies, but it is also about our actual lives. We have aches and pains in our physical bodies, but we have aches and pains in our lives lived here in this world, too. Make a list of what you learn.

This world -temporary "house"   His Kingdom- eternal "house"

Whose plan is this? How have we been prepared for this? What power source do we have?

How are we to walk out this life?

Why does this take courage?

Why is it important to learn to walk by faith and not by sight?

How does this happen?

We live in two worlds and they are competing for our devotion, faith, joy, hope and love. I can easily lean towards the one I see, towards pleasant circumstances, relationships, and self-love. And I can easily get discouraged when those things change or don't fill me up like I have hoped. Can you relate?

This is God's plan: in walking with us, drawing us, showing us our need and deeply healing our unbelief, great glory is given to His Name. This is God's way, and it's far above my own way. He is fully confident that His ways work and will be accomplished (see Philippians 1:6). He will do it and I have the opportunity to cooperate with His Spirit and grow in a love-based eternal relationship with the One who knows me. You have this opportunity, too.

Do we realize that this is all because we are loved? Not to be made loveable. We were loved while we were hopeless, lost, and dead. We were loved, first. Read these last texts and let the two kingdoms collide. Remember: His Kingdom wins.

As you read these verses, mark the word creation.

Romans 8:18–29

"18 For I consider that the sufferings of this present time are not worthy to be compared with the glory that is to be revealed to us. 19 For the anxious longing of the creation waits eagerly for the revealing of the sons of God. 20 For the creation was subjected to futility, not willingly, but because of Him who subjected it, in hope 21 that the creation itself also will be set free from its slavery to corruption into the freedom of the glory of the children of God. 22 For we know that the whole creation groans and suffers the pains of childbirth together until now."

Creation is personified in this text. What does this creation do?

Why do we look for our hope and healing in this world? What's the problem with that?

Mark the words groan and Holy Spirit in the following verses.

" 23 And not only this, but also we ourselves, having the first fruits of the Spirit, even we ourselves groan within ourselves, waiting eagerly for our adoption as sons, the redemption of our body. 24 For in hope we have been saved, but hope that is seen is not hope; for who hopes for what he already sees? 25 But if we hope for what we do not see, with perseverance we wait eagerly for it. 26 In the same way the Spirit also helps our weakness; for we do not know how to pray as we should, but the Spirit Himself intercedes for us with groanings too deep for words; 27 and He who searches the hearts knows what the mind of the Spirit is, because He intercedes for the saints according to the will of God."

What does the Spirit do? Why?

In these next verses, mark God and Christ and any pronouns.

"28 And we know that God causes all things to work together for good to those who love God, to those who are called according to His purpose. 29 For those whom He foreknew, He also predestined to become conformed to the image of His Son, so that He would be the firstborn among many brethren..."

What is God's eternal purpose for you?

In Christ Jesus you have been sealed by the Spirit, who was given to you as a deposit, a first fruit of whom you belong to. How does that strike your heart? What good is God working in you? For which kingdom?

In these verses, mark the references to God, Christ, (as well as any personal pronouns), and the word love.

Romans 8:31–39

"31 What then shall we say to these things? If God is for us, who is against us? 32 He who did not spare His own Son, but delivered Him over for us all, how will He not also with Him freely give us all things? 33 Who will bring a charge against God's elect? God is the one who justifies; 34 who is the one who condemns? Christ Jesus is He who died, yes, rather who was raised, who is at the right hand of God, who also intercedes for us. 35 Who will separate us from the love of Christ? Will tribulation, or distress, or persecution, or famine, or nakedness, or peril, or sword?

36 Just as it is written, 'For Your sake we are being put to death all day long; We were considered as sheep to be slaughtered.'"

37 But in all these things we overwhelmingly conquer through Him who loved us. 38 For I am convinced that neither death, nor life, nor angels, nor principalities, nor things present, nor things to come, nor powers, 39 nor height, nor depth, nor any other created thing, will be able to separate us from the love of God, which is in Christ Jesus our Lord."

What did God's love cost Him? What did it cost Jesus?

What was accomplished for you, in Christ?

Look at Romans 8:26 and 8:34. Who intercedes for you? How well do they know us and what we truly need for God's purposes to be accomplished in our lives?

Look up the word conquer (Greek Strong's number 5245).

We are fully loved, in Christ Jesus. What can separate us? Write out the list.

Now, is this a promise of complete seen victory in the temporary world we live in? In the world we see and experience every day? Why or why not?

In verse 37, underline the phrase, "But in these things…" Does that mean we will get out of them?

What are you convinced of? Do you tend to believe you are loved only if life is going well and if circumstances and people are good? I do. But I am incorrect in thinking and believing this way. These verses are true because they are true. Not because they look true or feel true. Write out Romans 8:38–39.

Seen by a Teen: *Only God could love us this much, because only God can conquer all these things. He conquers death and life, He knows and created all the angels, and He is greater than all the demons. He knows the present and the future. He has all power. He is greater than all heights and depths and nothing in all of creation can stand against Him. Nothing can separate us from His love.*

I am definitely feeling the fear of God, right now…the WOW fear of God. Nothing can compare to what these words mean…nothing. It's crazy, because in this society it's hard to love yourself and others but, in the Lord, all these things are effortless. He's done it. He is doing it. He's constantly pursuing us with His love. I wish I could love Him and others the same in return...the only way to do that is to grow in this love, and that is by growing in the love of Spirit.

Ponder: Well, this is our last week together and I purposely made it a "big picture" week! I can only pray, right now...

Search me, Lord! Show me, what holds me back from fully trusting You? Examine and show me how my anxious thought are really rooted in some kind of unbelief in You, Your character, or Your ways...increase my faith!

Expose, for Your purposes, my sin and unbelief all the way down to my attitudes, motives and thinking patterns—even to my feeling patterns. SO much is rooted in my wounds and only You know and understand!

You came to heal and redeem. I don't even understand what that truly means, Lord...but You do! Use your Word. Give me a hunger to know You, Your Word, and accept the ways it penetrates so deeply.

Thank You that this world is not our home, our hope, or our joy. Thank You that we are being prepared for a better place, where sin and sorrow are no more. Where we will be in Your image, as our individual part of Your One Body, Your One Bride. Teach me to walk by faith and not by sight because I am loved. Grow me up in Your love! Teach me to trust Your love that I may walk as a conqueror, in the midst of the mess."

What about you? How has the Lord's Word penetrated you? What is He exposing? How is He healing? Have you heard Him call your name, beloved? Be still. Listen.

Seen by a Teen *[Question: As a teenager, where is your biggest struggle to find security and love? How would you encourage another teen to look for their value in Jesus?]*

Where do I look for love and security? Probably myself. Not only do other people fail us but most of the time we also end up failing ourselves. We put expectations on ourselves that we can't meet, like perfection. Now, I know I can't be perfect so where on earth am I going to find a person that I can trust in? I've tried myself, my parents, my friends and even a boyfriend. All of them have failed, including myself, and we keep failing. Jesus really is the only option. That's why I need to continue to remember the truth, to study God's Word, pray and seek out others who are following Jesus and keep on keeping on...

Pulling Together: If you have time, read over the texts of the week one more time and consider the following questions:

•   What do you learn about the character of God—Father, Son, and Spirit—in the texts of the week?

•   Is there a thread of the hope of the Gospel in the text? Where do you see it?

•   Is there a window into the human heart? What is it? What do you learn about yourself and about other people relative to you?

•   Where do you need to stop, consider, pray, receive Truth or walk in faith? Write down what He is showing you to do.

🄰

Keepsakes: This is our last verse of the week. Keep treasuring the Word of God—it is priceless! Write out the verse of the week at least two times. Write out all four weeks' verses if you can!

Psalm 139:24, "And see if there be any hurtful way in me, and lead me in the everlasting way."

Sharing Your Heart: In our final week together, look over the previous weeks and see what the Lord has shown you. Spend a little time either praying, journaling or perhaps singing in worship about Who He is and what He has done!

Lord, I praise you because You are…

Thank you, O Lord, that you know…that you Are…that you Are doing…

I bend my heart, my knees, and my life to You because…

Reach Out: Take some time this week and write a note of encouragement to someone who needs to be reminded of God's love for them or the fact that He has a plan and that is good. Pray for them and trust the Lord with them!

Notes: Week 4